D1107849

This book is a presentation of Weekly Reader
Books. Weekly Reader Books offers book
clubs for children from preschool through high
school. For further information write to:
WEEKLY READER BOOKS, 4343 Equity Drive,
Columbus, Ohio 43228

This edition is published by arrangement
with Checkerboard Press.

WEEKLY READER BOOKS presents

What Is a Vegetable?

A **Just Ask**™ Book

Hi, my name is
Christopher!

by Chris Arvetis
and Carole Palmer

illustrated by
Vernon McKissack

FIELD PUBLICATIONS
MIDDLETOWN, CT.

VEG-E-TA-BLE—
what is a vegetable?

Vegetables are special parts of certain plants that we eat at mealtime or for a snack.

We can eat the leaves, stems, flowers, roots or seeds.

From some plants we eat
the leaves.
We will eat the leaves
of this plant.
It is lettuce.
There are many kinds
of lettuce.

LETTUCE

We also eat the leaves of these plants—cabbage, spinach, cress, mustard, and parsley.

SPINACH

CABBAGE

Look at these plants.
Here we eat the stems.
The plants are asparagus
and rhubarb.

ASPARAGUS

These vegetables are hiding!
We don't eat the parts we see.
We eat the roots or the stems
that grow underground.
See the white potatoes
and sweet potatoes?
And there are carrots, beets,
turnips, and radishes.

BEET

TURNIP

Sometimes we eat just
the seeds of plants.
Lima beans and peas are two
plants whose seeds we eat.

PEAS

We eat the seeds of corn, too.
Corn grows on cobs, and the
seeds are called kernels.
There is white corn
and yellow corn.

Look at the round, red tomato
growing on that plant.

We eat the seeds inside
a tomato.

We also eat the soft part
around the seeds.

The whole tomato is the part
of the plant called the *fruit*.

A tomato is usually called
a vegetable because it does
not taste as sweet as many
fruits do.

Cucumbers, squashes,
and peppers grow
like tomatoes.
They all have seeds.
Pumpkins do, too.

We eat the flower parts
of some plants.
Broccoli and cauliflower are
two of those vegetables.

CAULIFLOWER

Now you know what kinds
of vegetables there are.
Vegetables help our bodies
grow and stay healthy.
Vegetables have vitamins.
Vegetables have vitamin A,
vitamin B, vitamin C,
iron and many more.

Everyone should eat potatoes and green, leafy vegetables and yellow vegetables.